Bhagavad Gita

A. M. Sastri

Edited by Amit Shah

ISBN: 9798665062136

DEDICATION

To my wife

CONTENTS

ACKNOWLEDGMENTS

The Bhagavad Gita was written about 200BCE and originally commented by Sri Shankaracharya. Alladi Mahadeva Sastri translated the Sanskrit commentaries by Sri Shankaracharya in 1901.

Alladi Mahadeva Sastri (1861-1926) was born in Pudur, India. Being well studied in Sanskrit and English, he was able to recite the Vedas at a young age.

In 1891 he became the first Curator of the Oriental Library and began translating the classic Bhagavat Gita commentaries by Sri Shankaracharya into English. He was praised by Swami Vivekananda for this commendable work. Sastri book was published in 1901.

The work is comparable, if not better, to other translations and gives precise translations of difficult Sanskrit words.

In editing this book, I have removed all the commentaries and kept just the sloka translations. Also removed the 'old English' to make the verses more palatable to the modern English. This allows for fluid reading of passages.

1 – DESPONDENCY OF ARJUNA

Sanjaya narrates the course of the war

Dhritarashtra said:

1. Samjaya, what did the Pandu's sons and mine do when they assembled on the sacred plain of Kurukshetra eager for battle?

Samjaya said:

2. Dhritarashtra, having seen the army of the Pandavas drawn up in battle-array, prince Duryodhana then approached his teacher and spoke (these) words:

Duryodhana addresses Drona

3. Teacher, look at this grand army of the sons of Pandu, marshalled by your talented pupil, the son of Drupada.

4. Here are heroes, mighty archers, equal in battle to Bhima and Arjuna, — Yuyudhana, Virata, and Drupada,

5. Dhrishtaketu, Chekitana, and the valiant king of Kasi, Purujit and Kunti-Bhoja and Saibya;

6. The heroic Yudhamanyu and the brave Uttamaujas; the son of Subhadra and the sons of Draupadi.

7. But know, the leaders of my army; these I name to by way of example.

8. Yourself and Bhishma, and Karna, and also Kripa, the victor in war, Asvatthaman and Vikarna, and also Jayadratha, the son of Somadatta;

9. And many other heroes who have given up their lives for my sake, fighting with various weapons, all well-skilled in battle.

10. This army of ours protected by Bhishma is inadequate, whereas that army of theirs which is under the protection of Bhima is adequate.

11. And therefore everyone occupying your respective positions in the several divisions of the army, support Bhishma only.

Both armies ready for battle.

12. The mighty Bhishma sounded on high a lion's roar and blew his conch.

13. Then, all at once, conches and kettledrums, cymbals, drums, and horns were played upon, and the sound was a tumultuous uproar.

14. Then, too, Madhava and the son of Pandu, seated in a grand chariot yoked to white horses, blew their celestial conches.

15. Hrishtkesa blew the Panchajanya, and Arjuna blew the Devadatta. Bhima blew his great conch Paundra.

16. Prince Yudhishthira, the son of Kunti, blew the

Anantavijaya, while Nakula and Sahadeva blew the Sughosha and the Manipushpaka.

17. The king of Kasi, an excellent archer, Sikhandin, Dhrishtadyumna and Virata, and the unconquered Satyaki;

18. Drupada and the sons of Draupadi, and the son of Subhadra all blew their respective conches.

19. That tumultuous sound rent the hearts of (the people) of Dhritarashtra's party, making both heaven and earth resound.

Arjuna's survey of the enemy.

20-22. Then seeing the people of Dhritarashtra's party regularly marshalled, while the discharge of weapons began, Arjuna, the son of Pandu, whose ensign was a monkey, took up his bow and said thus to Krishna:

"O Achyuta (Immortal), place my chariot between the two armies, that I may just see those who stand here desirous to fight, and know with whom I must fight in this strife of battle.

23. "I will observe those who are assembled here and are about to engage in battle desirous to do service in war to the evil-minded son of Dhritarashtra"

Samjaya said:

24-25. Hrishikesa (Krishna) thus addressed by Guiakesa (Arjuna) stationed between the two armies in front of Bhishma and Drona and all the rulers of earth, and said: "O son of Pritha, look at these assembled Kauravas."

26-27. Then the son of Pritha saw arrayed there in both the armies fathers and grandfathers, teachers, maternal uncles, brothers, sons, grand- sons and comrades, fathers-in-law and friends.

27-28. When Arjuna saw all the kinsmen standing, he was overcome with deepest pity and said thus in sorrow:

Arjuna's words of despondency.

Arjuna said:

28-29. Seeing these kinsmen, O Krishna, arrayed and desirous to fight, my limbs droop down, and my mouth is dried up. A tremor comes on my body and my hairs stand on end.

30. The Gandiva slips from my hand, and my skin is intensely burning. I am also unable to stand and my mind is whirling round.

31. And, I see omens foreboding evil. Nor do I see any good from killing my kinsmen in battle.

32. I desire not victory, nor kingdom, nor pleasures. Of what avail is dominion to us? Of what avail are pleasures and even life?

33-34. They for whose sake dominion, enjoyments and pleasures are sought by us are here standing, having staked their life and wealth: teachers, fathers, sons as well as grandfathers; maternal uncles, fathers-in-law, grandsons, brothers-in-law as also (other) relatives.

35. These I do not wish to kill, though they kill me, even for the sake of dominion over the three worlds; how much less for the sake of the earth!

36. What delight shall be ours after killing the sons of Dhritarashtra? On killing these felons, sin only will take hold

of us.

37. We had then better not slay our own kinsmen, the sons of Dhritarashtra; for, how can we be happy after slaying our own people?

Arjun's grief at the evils of war

38-39. Though these, whose intelligence is stricken by greed, perceive no evil in the extinction of families and no sin in treachery to friends, yet, should not we, who clearly see evil in the extinction of a family, learn to refrain from this sinful deed?

40. On the extinction of a family, the immemorial dharmas of that family disappear. When the dharmas disappear, impiety (adharma) overtakes the whole family.

41. By the prevalence of impiety, the women of the family become corrupt. Women corrupted, there will be intermingling of castes.

42. Confusion of castes leads the family of these destroyers of families also to hell; for, their forefathers fall (down to hell), deprived of the offerings of pinda and water.

43. By these evil deeds of the destroyers of families which cause the intermingling of castes, the eternal dharmas of castes and families are subverted.

44. We have heard, that necessary is the dwelling in hell of the men whose family dharmas are subverted.

45. Alas! We have resolved to commit a great sin, because we are endeavoring to slay our kinsmen out of a craving for the pleasures of dominion.

46. It would be better for me, if the sons of Dhritarashtra,

with arms in hand, should slay me unarmed and unresisting in the battle.

Samjaya said:

47. Having said thus, Arjuna, sorrow-stricken in mind, cast aside his bow and arrows during the battle and sat down in the chariot.

2 - SANKHYA YOGA (Yoga of Knowledge)

Arjunas weakness condemned by the Lord

1. To him who was thus overcome with pity and afflicted, and whose eyes were full of tears and agitated, the destroyer of Madhu spoke as follows:

The Lord said:

2. Whence in (this) perilous strait has come upon you this weakness cherished by the unworthy, debarring from heaven and causing disgrace, Arjuna?

3. Yield not to unmanliness. It does not become you. Cast off this base weakness of heart and arise.

Arjuna seeks instruction from the Lord

Arjuna said:

4. Krishna, how shall I assail in battle with arrows Bhishma and Drona, who are worthy of worship.

5. Better indeed in this world to live even upon alms than to slay the teachers of high honor. But, were I to slay these teachers, I should only in this world enjoy the pleasures of

wealth, delights stained with blood.

6. And we know not which is the better alternative for us; nor do we know whether we shall conquer them, or they will conquer us. Even the sons of Dhritarashtra, after killing whom we do not wish to live, stand arrayed against us.

7. My heart contaminated by the taint of helplessness, my mind confounded about Dharma, I ask you: Tell me what is good. I am your pupil. Instruct me, who have sought your grace.

8. I do not indeed see what can dispel the grief which burns up my senses, even after attaining unrivalled and prosperous dominion on earth or even lordship over gods.

Samjaya said:

9. Having spoken thus to Krishna, Arjuna said to Krishna, ' I will not fight,' and verily remained silent.

10. To him who was grieving amid the two armies, Krishna as if smiling, spoke these words: Self-knowledge alone eradicates misery.

The Lord said:

11. For those who deserve no grief you have grieved, and words of wisdom you speak. For the living and the dead, the wise grieve not.

12. Never did I not exist, nor you, nor these rulers of men; and no one of us will ever hereafter cease to exist.

13. Just as in this body the embodied (Self) passes into childhood and youth and old age, so does He pass into another body. There the wise man is not distressed.

Endurance is a condition of wisdom

14. The sense-contacts it is which cause heat and cold, pleasure and pain; they come and go, they are impermanent. Them endure bravely, Arjuna.

15. That wise man whom, verily, these afflict not to whom pleasure and pain are same, he for immortality is fit.

The Real and the Unreal

16. Of the unreal no being there is; there is no non-being of the real. Of both these is the truth seen by the seers of the Essence.

17. But know that to be imperishable by which all this is pervaded. None can cause the destruction of That, the Inexhaustible.

18. These bodies of the embodied (Self) who is eternal, indestructible, and unknowable, are said to have an end. Do fight, therefore, Arjuna.

The Self is unconcerned in action

19. Whoever looks upon Him as the slayer, and whoever looks upon Him as the slain, both these know not aright. He slays not, nor is He slain.

The Self is immutable

20. He is not born, nor does He ever die; after having been, He again ceases not to be; nor the reverse. Unborn, eternal, unchangeable, and primeval, He is not slain when the body is slain.

The enlightened man must renounce works

21. Whoso knows Him as indestructible, eternal, unborn, and inexhaustible, — How, Arjuna, and whom, does such a man cause to slay, and whom does he slay?

How the Self is immutable

22. Just as a man casts off worn-out clothes and puts on others which are new, so the embodied (Self) casts off worn-out bodies and enters others which are new.

23. Him, weapons cut not; Him, fire burns not, and Him, water wets not; Him, wind dries not.

24. He cannot be cut, nor burnt, nor wetted, nor dried up. He is everlasting, all-pervading, stable, firm, and eternal.

No room for grief

25. He, it is said, is unmanifest, unthinkable and unchangeable. Wherefore, knowing Him to be such, you should not grieve.

26. But even if you think of Him as ever being born and ever dying, even then, Arjuna, you should not grieve.

27. To that which is born, death is indeed certain; and to that which is dead, birth is certain. Wherefore, about the unavoidable thing, you should not grieve.

28. Beings have their beginning unseen, their middle seen, and their end unseen again. Why any lamentation regarding them?

29. One sees Him as a wonder; and so also another speaks of Him as a wonder; and as a wonder another hears of Him; and though hearing, none understands Him at all.

30. He, the embodied (Self) in every one's body, can never be killed, Arjuna. Wherefore you should not grieve about any creature.

A warrior should flight

31. Having regard to thine own duty also, you should not

waver. For, to a Kshatriya, there is nothing more wholesome than a lawful battle.

32. Happy Kshatriya find such a battle as this, come of itself, an open door to heaven.

33. Now if you wouldst not fight this lawful battle, then, having abandoned thine own duty and fame, you shalt incur sin.

34. People, too, will recount your everlasting infamy; and, to one who has been esteemed, infamy is more than death.

35 The great car-warriors will think you have withdrawn from the battle through fear; and, having been (hitherto) highly esteemed by them, you will incur their contempt.

36 Your enemies, too, scorning your power, will talk many abusive words. What is more painful than that?

37. Killed, you will reach heaven; victorious, you will enjoy the earth. Wherefore, Arjuna, arise, resolved to fight.

38. Then, treating alike pleasure and pain, gain and loss, success, and defeat, prepare for the battle, and you will not incur sin.

Yoga

39. This, which has been taught to you, is wisdom concerning Sankhya. Now, listen to wisdom concerning Yoga, which possessing you shalt cast off the bond of action.

Yoga, a safe course

40. There is no loss of effort here, there is no harm. Even a little of this devotion delivers one from great fear.

Wisdom is one

41. Here, Arjuna, there is one thought of a resolute nature. Many branched and endless are the thoughts of the irresolute.

No wisdom possible for the worldly-minded

42-44. No conviction of a resolute nature is formed in the mind of those who are attached to pleasures and power, and whose minds are drawn away by that flowery speech which the unwise — enamored of Vedic utterances, declaring there is nothing else, full of desire, having svarga as their goal — utter, (a speech) which promises birth as the reward of actions and which abounds in specific acts for the attainment of pleasure and power, Arjuna.

Advice to the Yogin

45. The Vedas treat of the triad of the gunas. Be free from the triad of the gunas, free from pairs, free from acquisition and preservation, ever remaining in Sattva (Goodness), and self-possessed.

Karma-Yoga

46. What utility there is in a reservoir (as compared) with an all-spreading flood of water, the same (utility) there is in all Vedas for an enlightened Brahma

47. Your concern is with action alone, never with results. Let not the fruit of action be your motive, nor let your attachment for inaction.

48. Steadfast in devotion do your works, casting off attachment, being the same in success and failure. Evenness is called Yoga.

49. Verily action is far inferior to devotion in wisdom (buddhi-yoga). In wisdom (buddhi) seek your shelter.

Wretched are they whose motive is the fruit.

Merits of wisdom

50. He who is endued with wisdom casts off here both good deeds and bad deeds. Wherefore apply yourself to devotion. Regarding actions devotion is a power.

Results of Karma-Yoga

51. For, men of wisdom cast off the fruit of action; possessed of knowledge (and) released from the bond of birth, they go to the place where there is no evil.

52. When your mind shall cross beyond the mire of delusion, then will you attain to a disgust of what is yet to be heard and what has been heard.

53. When your mind, perplexed by what you have heard, shall stand firm and steady in the Self, then will you attain Yoga.

The characteristic attributes of a perfect sage

Arjuna said:

54. What, Krishna, is the description of one of steady knowledge, who is constant in contemplation? How does one of steady knowledge speak, how sit, how move?

55. When a man, satisfied in the Self alone by himself, completely casts off all the desires of the mind, then is he said to be one of steady knowledge.

56. He whose heart is not distressed in calamities, from whom all longing for pleasures has departed, who is free from attachment, fear, and wrath, he is called a sage, a man of steady know- ledge.

57. Whoso, without attachment anywhere, on meeting with

anything good or bad, neither exults nor hates, his knowledge becomes steady.

58. When he completely withdraws the senses from sense-objects, as the tortoise (withdraws) its limbs from all sides, his knowledge is steady.

59. Objects withdraw from an abstinent man, but not the taste. On 'seeing the Supreme, his taste, too, ceases.

Unrestraint sense work mischief

60. The dangerous senses forcibly carry away the mind of a wise man, even while striving (to control them).

61. Restraining them all, a man should remain steadfast, intent on Me. His knowledge is steady whose senses are under control.

Thought of sense-objects is the source of evil

62. When a man thinks of objects, attachment for them arises. From attachment arises desire; from desire arises wrath.

63. From wrath arises delusion; from delusion, failure of memory; from failure of memory, loss of conscience; from loss of conscience he is utterly ruined.

Sense-control leads to peace and happiness

64. He attains peace, who, self-controlled, approaches objects with senses devoid of love and hatred and brought under his own control.

65. In peace there is an end of all his miseries; for, the reason of the tranquil-minded soon becomes steady.

66. There is no wisdom to the unsteady, and no meditation to the unsteady, and to the unmeditative no peace; to the

peaceless, how can there be happiness?

Sense-restraint conduces to steady knowledge

67. For, the mind which yields to the roving senses carries away his knowledge, as the wind (carries away) a ship on water.

68. Therefore, Arjuna, his knowledge is steady whose senses have been entirely restrained from sense-objects.

69. What is night to all beings, therein the self-controlled one is awake. Where all beings are awake, that is the night of the sage who sees.

70. He attains peace, into whom all desires enter as waters enter the ocean, which, filled from all sides, remains unaltered; but not he who desires objects.

71. That man attains peace, who, abandoning all desires, moves about without attachment, without selfishness, without vanity.

Knowledge leads to Divine Felicity

72. This is the Brahmic state, Arjuna. Attaining to this, none is deluded. Remaining in this state even at the last period of life, one attains to the felicity of Brahman

3 - KARMA-YOGA (Yoga of Action)

Which is better, knowledge or action

Arjuna said:

1. If it be thought by you that knowledge is superior to action, Krishna, why then do you direct me to this terrible action?

2. With an apparently perplexing speech, you confuse my understanding. Tell me with certainty that one (way) by which I may attain bliss.

The paths of knowledge and action

The Blessed Lord said:

3. In this world a twofold path was taught by Me at first, Arjuna: that of the Sankhyas by devotion to knowledge, and that of the yogins by devotion to action.

4. Not by abstaining from action does man win actionlessness, nor by mere renunciation does he attain perfection.

The ignorant are swayed by Nature

5. None, verily, even for an instant, ever remains doing no

action; for everyone is driven helpless to action by the energies born of Nature.

The unenlightened should not give up Karma-Yoga

6. He who, restraining the organs of action, sits thinking in his mind of the objects of the sense? self-deluded, he is said to be one of false conduct.

7. But whoso, restraining the senses by mind, Arjuna, engages in Karma-Yoga, unattached, with organs of action, he is esteemed.

Wherefore,

8. Do perform your bounden duty; for, action is superior to inaction. And even the maintenance of the body would not be possible for you by inaction.

9. Except in the case of action for Sacrifice's sake, this world is action-bound. Action for the sake Thereof, do thou, Arjuna, perform, free from attachment.

10. Having first created mankind together with sacrifices, the Prajapati said, “By this shall you propagate; let this be to you the cow of plenty”.

11. With this nourishes the Gods, and the Gods shall nourish you; thus nourishing one another, you shall attain the supreme good.

12. Nourished by the sacrifice, the Gods shall indeed bestow on you the enjoyments your desire. “Who enjoys — without offering to Them — Their gifts, he is verily a thief”.

On the other hand,

13. The righteous, who eat the remnant of the sacrifice, are freed from all sins; but sin do the impious eat who cook for

their own sakes.

The wheel of the world should be set-going

14-15. From food creatures come forth; the production of food is from rain; rain comes forth from sacrifice; sacrifice is born of action; know that action comes from Brahman and that Brahman comes from the Imperishable. Therefore, the all-pervading Brahman ever resets in sacrifice.

16. He who follows not here the wheel thus set in motion, who is of sinful life, indulging in senses, he lives in vain, Arjuna.

17. That man, verily, who rejoices only in the Self, who is satisfied with the Self, who is content in the Self alone, — for him there is nothing to do.

18. For him, there is here no interest whatever in what is done or what is not done. Nor is there in all beings any one he should resort to for I any object.

Arjuna qualified for Karma-Yoga

19 Therefore, without attachment, constantly perform the action which should be done; for, per- forming action without attachment, man reaches the Supreme.

The wise should set an example to the masses

For the following reason also (you should perform action):

20 By action only, indeed, did Janaka and others try to attain perfection. Even with a view to the protection of the masses you should perform (action).

21. Whatsoever a great man does, that alone the other men do; whatever he sets up as the standard, that the world follows.

22 I have nothing whatsoever to achieve in the three worlds, Arjuna, nor is there any- thing unattained that should be attained; yet I engage in action. I have nothing to achieve, for, there is nothing unattained.

23. For, should I not ever engage in action, unwearied, men would in all matters follow My path, Arjuna.

24. These worlds would be ruined if I should not perform action; I should be the cause of confusion of castes and should destroy these creatures.

The wise man's action as contrasted with that of the ignorant

25. As ignorant men act attached to work, so should the wise man act, unattached, from a wish to protect the masses.

26. Let no wise man cause unsettlement in the minds of the ignorant who are attached to action; he should make them do all actions, himself fulfilling them with devotion.

In what way is an ignorant man attached to actions?

27. Actions are wrought in all cases by the energies of Nature. He whose mind is deluded by egoism thinks ' I am the doer.'

But as regards the wise man:

28. But he who knows the truth, Arjuna, about the divisions of the energies and (their) functions, is not attached, thinking that the energies act upon the energies.

29. Those deluded by the energies of Nature are attached to the functions of the energies. He who knows the All should not unsettle the unwise who know not the All.

How an aspirant for Moksha should do actions

30. Renouncing all actions in Me, with your thought resting on the Self, being free from hope, free from selfishness, devoid of fever, do you fight.

31. Men who constantly practice this teaching of Mine with faith and without caviling, they too are liberated from actions.

32. But those who, carping at this, My teaching, practice it not, — know them as deluded in all know- ledge, as senseless men doomed to destruction.

Influence of man's nature on his conduct

33. Even the man of knowledge acts in conformity with his own nature; (all) beings follow (their) nature; what shall coercion avail?

Scope for man's personal exertion

The Lord replies as follows:

34. Love and hate lie towards the object of each sense; let none become subject to these two; for they are his enemies.

35. Better one's own duty, though devoid of merit, than the duty of another well discharged. Better is death in one's own duty; the duty of another is productive of danger.

Desire is the enemy of man

Arjuna said:

36. But by what dragged on, Krishna, does a man, though reluctant, commit sin, as if constrained by force?

The Blessed Lord said:

37. It is Desire, it is Wrath, born of the energy of Rajas, all-

devouring, all-sinful; that, know thou, is the foe here.

Desire enshrouds wisdom

38. As fire is surrounded by smoke, as a mirror by dust, as the fetus is enclosed in the womb, so is this covered by it.

39. Covered, Arjuna, is wisdom by this constant enemy of the wise, in the form of desire, which is greedy and insatiable.

The seat of desire

40. The senses, mind, and reason are said to be its seat; veiling wisdom through these, it deludes the embodied.

How to kill out desire

Wherefore,

41. Therefore, Arjuna, restrain the senses first, cast off this sinful thing which is destructive of knowledge and wisdom.

42. They say that the senses are superior; superior to the senses is mind; superior to mind is reason; one who is even superior to reason is He.

43. Thus knowing Him who is superior to reason, subduing the self by the self, slay the enemy in the form of desire.

4 – JNANA-YOGA (Yoga of Renunciation of Action through Knowledge)

Tradition of Jnana-Yoga

The Blessed Lord said:

1. I taught this imperishable Yoga to Vivasvat; Vivasvat taught it to Manu; Manu taught it to Ikshvaku.

2. This, handed down thus in succession, the King-sages learnt. This Yoga, by long lapse of time, has been lost here, Arjuna.

3. That same ancient Yoga has been today taught to you by Me, seeing that you are My devotee and friend; for, this is the Supreme Secret.

Divine Incarnations

4. Later is your birth, and prior the birth of Vivasvat; how am I to understand that you taught this Yoga in the beginning?

The Blessed Lord said:

5. Many births of Mine have passed, as well as of yours,

Arjuna; all these I know, you do not know.

6. Though I am unborn, of imperishable nature, and though I am the Lord of all beings, yet ruling over My own nature, I am born by My own Maya.

7. Whenever there is a decay of religion and an ascendency of irreligion, then I manifest Myself.

8. For the protection of the good, for the destruction of evil doers, for the firm establishment of religion, I am born in every age.

9. Whoso knows thus My divine birth and action in truth is not born again on leaving this body; he comes to Me.

Jnana-Yoga is the sole means to moksha

10. Free from passion, fear, and anger, absorbed in Me, taking refuge in Me, purified by the fire (tapas) of wisdom, many have reached My being.

11. Howsoever men approach Me, even so do I reward them; My path do men follow in all things.

12. They who long after success in actions sacrifice here to the Gods; for, soon in this world of man accrues success from action.

13. The fourfold caste has been created by Me according to the distribution of energies and actions; though I am the author thereof, know Me as non-agent and immutable.

Action without attachment does not bind the soul

14. Actions pollute Me not, nor have I a desire for the fruit of actions. He who knows Me thus is not bound by actions.

15. Thus knowing, men of old performed action in the hope

of liberation; therefore you also perform action as did the ancients in the olden time.

The real nature of action and inaction

16. What is action? What is inaction? — As to this, even the wise are deluded. I shall teach you such action, by knowing which you shalt be liberated from evil.

17. For, you have to know something even of action, something to know of unlawful action, and something to know of inaction; hard to under- stand is the nature of action.

18. He who can see inaction in action, who can also see action in inaction, he is wise among men, he is devout, he is the performer of all action.

Who is a sage?

19. He whose engagements are all devoid of desires and purposes, and whose actions have been burnt by the fire of wisdom, him the wise call a sage.

The sage's worldly action as an example to the masses

20. Having abandoned attachment for the fruits of action, ever content, dependent on none, though engaged in actions, nothing at all does he do.

The sage's action for bodily maintenance

21. Free from desire, with the mind and the self-controlled, having relinquished all possessions, doing mere bodily action, he incurs no sin.

22. Satisfied with what comes to him by chance, rising above the pairs of opposites, free from envy, equanimous in success and failure, though acting he is not bound.

The sage's worldly action does not bind him

Lord Says:

23. Of the man whose attachment is gone, who is liberated, whose mind is established in knowledge, who acts for the sake of sacrifice, — his whole action melts away.

Wisdom-sacrifice

24. Brahman is the offering, Brahman the oblation; by Brahman is the oblation poured into the fire of Brahman; Brahman verily shall be reached by him who always sees Brahman in action.

25. Other yogins resort to sacrifices to Gods; in the fire of Brahman others offer the Self by the Self.

26. Others offer hearing and other senses in the fires of restraint; others offer sound and other objects in the fires of the senses.

27. And others sacrifice all the functions of the senses and the functions of the vitality in the wisdom-kindled fire of the Yoga of Self-restraint.

28. Others are sacrificers by their wealth, sacriticers by austerity, sacrilicers by Yogas, sacrificers by reading and knowledge, ascetics of rigid vows.

29. Others offer prana (outgoing breath) in apana (incoming breath), and apana in prana, restraining the passages of prana and apana, absorb ed in pranayama (restraint of breath).

30. Others, with regulated food, offer life-breaths in life-breaths. All these are knowers of sacrifice, whose sins are destroyed by sacrifice.

31. Eating of ambrosia, the remnant of the sacrifice, they go to Eternal Brahman. This world is not for the non-sacrificer; whence the other? Arjuna.

32. Thus manifold sacrifices are spread at the mouth of Brahman. Know them all as born of action. Thus knowing, you shall be liberated.

Wisdom-sacrifice is superior to other sacrifices

33. Superior is wisdom-sacrifice to the sacrifice with objects. All action, without exception is comprehended in wisdom.

How and where one should seek wisdom

34. Know this: by long prostration, by enquiry, by service, those men of wisdom who have realized the truth will teach you wisdom.

35. Knowing which, you shall not again thus fall into error; and by which, you will see all beings in your Self and also in Me.

Wisdom, a consumer of all sins and actions

36. Even if you are the most sinful of all the sinful, you shall verily cross all sin by the boat of wisdom.

37. As kindled fire reduces fuel to ashes, so does wisdom-fire reduce all actions to ashes.

38. Verily, there exists here no purifier equal to wisdom. He who is perfected by Yoga finds it in time in himself by himself.

The surest means to wisdom

39. He obtains wisdom who is fall of faith, who is devoted to it, and who has subdued the senses. Having obtained wisdom, he ere long attains to the Supreme Peace.

Wisdom the killer of doubt

40. The ignorant, the faithless, and one of doubting self, is ruined. There is neither this world, nor the other, nor happiness, for one of doubting self.

41. Him who has renounced actions by Yoga, whose doubts have been cloven asunder by wisdom, who is self-possessed, actions bind not.

42. Therefore with the sword of wisdom cleave asunder this doubt of the Self lying in the heart and born of ignorance, and resort to Yoga. Arise, Arjuna.

5 - SAMNYASA-YOGA (Yoga of Renunciation)

Which is better for the ignorant, Karma-Yoga or Samnyasa?

Arjuna said:

1. You praise renunciation of actions and Yoga. Tell me conclusively that which is the better of the two.

Karma-Yoga suites the ignorant better than Samnyasa

The Blessed Lord said:

2. Renunciation and Yoga through action both lead to the highest bliss; but, of the two. Yoga through action is esteemed more than renunciation of action.

3. He should be known as a perpetual renouncer who neither hates nor desires; for, free from the pairs of opposites, he is easily set free from bondage

Sankhya and Yoga lead to the same goal

4. Children, not the wise, speak of Sankhya and Yoga as distinct. He who is rightly devoted to even one obtains the fruits of both.

5. That state which is reached by Sankhyas is reached by

Yogins also. He sees, who sees Sankhya and Yoga as one.

Karma-Yoga is a means to Samnyasa

6. But renunciation is hard to attain except by Yoga; a sage equipped with Yoga ere long reaches Brahman.

A sage's actions do not affect him

7. He who is equipped with Yoga, whose mind is quite pure, by whom the self has been conquered, whose senses have been subdued, whose Self has become the Self of all beings, — though doing, he is not tainted.

A sage's actions are really no actions

8-9. 'I do nothing at all'; thus should the truth- knower think, steadfast, — though seeing, hearing, touching, smelling, eating, going, sleeping, breathing, speaking, letting go, seizing, opening and closing the eyes, — remembering that the senses move among sense-objects.

Karma-Yogin is untainted by the results of his action

10. He who does actions, offering them to Brahman, abandoning attachment, is not tainted by sin, as a lotus leaf by water.

11. By the body, by the mind, by, the intellect, by mere senses also, Yogins perform action, without attachment, for the purification of the self.

12. The steady-minded one, abandoning the fruit of action, attains the peace born of devotion. The unsteady one, attached to the fruit through the action of desire, is firmly bound.

The blissful embodied life of a sage

13. Renouncing all actions by thought, and Self-controlled, the embodied one rests happily in the nine-gated city,

neither at all acting nor causing to act.

Nature is the source of activity

14. Neither agency nor objects does the Lord create for the world, nor union with the fruits of actions. But it is the nature that acts.

Wisdom and unwisdom

15. The Lord takes neither the evil nor even the good deed of any; wisdom is enveloped by unwisdom; thereby mortals are deluded.

16. But to those whose unwisdom is destroyed by wisdom of the Self, like the sun wisdom illuminates that Supreme.

Sage has no more births

17. With their consciousness in That, their Self being That, intent on That, with That for their supreme goal, they go never again to return, their sins shaken off by means of wisdom.

The sage sees the One in all beings

18. In a Brahmana endued with wisdom and humility, in a cow, in an elephant, as also in a dog and in a dog-eater, the wise see the same.

The sage is liberated while still on earth

19. Even here birth is overcome by them whose mind rests on equality. Spotless, indeed, and equal is Brahman; wherefore in Brahman they rest.

The sage is free from grief and rejoicing

20. He who knows Brahman can neither rejoice on obtaining the pleasant, nor grieve on obtaining the unpleasant, — steady-minded, undeluded, resting in Brahman.

The sage's infinite joy

21. With the self-unattached to external contacts, he finds the joy which is in the Self; with the Self engaged in the contemplation of Brahman he attains the endless joy.

22. For, those delights which arc born of contacts are only generators of pain, having a beginning and an end; a wise man rejoices not in them.

The path of Nirvana

23. He that is able, while still here, to withstand, before liberation from the body, the impulse of desire and anger, he is a Yogin, he is a happy man.

24. Whoso has his joy within and his pastime within, and whoso has his light within only, that Yogin attains Brahman's bliss, himself becoming Brahman.

25. The sages attain Brahman's bliss, — they whose sins have been destroyed and doubts removed, who are self-controlled and intent on the welfare of all beings.

26. To the devotees who are free from desire and anger, who have controlled their thought, and who have known the Self, Brahman's bliss exists everywhere.

Realization of the Lord by Dhyana-Yoga

27-28. Shutting out all external contacts and fixing the sight between the eye-brows, equalizing the out-going and the in-going breaths which pass through the nostrils, controlling the senses, mind and intellect, having moksha as his highest goal, free from desire, fear and anger, — the sage who ever (remains thus) is verily liberated.

29. On knowing Me, — the Lord of all sacrifices and austerities, the Great Lord of all worlds, the friend of all

beings — he goes to Peace.

6 – DHYANA-YOGA (Yoga of Meditation)

Renunciation in action

The Blessed Lord said:

1. He who, without depending on the fruits of action, performs his bounden duty, he is a Samnyasin and a Yogin; not he who is without fire and without action.

2. Do you know Yoga to be that which they call renunciation; no one, verily, becomes a Yogin who has not renounced thoughts.

Action is a stepping-stone to Dhyana-Yoga

3. For a devotee who wishes to attain to Yoga, action is said to be the means. For the same (devotee), when he has attained to Yoga, quiescence (sama) is said to be the means.

4. When a man, renouncing all thoughts, is not attached to sense-objects and actions, then he is said to have attained to Yoga.

5. Let a man raise himself by himself, let him not lower himself; for, he alone is the friend of himself, he alone is the

enemy of himself.

6. To him who has conquered himself by himself, his own self is the friend of himself, but, to him who has not (conquered) himself, his own self stands in the place of an enemy like the (external) foe.

7. The self-controlled and serene man's Supreme Self is steadfast in cold and heat, in pleasure and pain, as also in honor and disgrace.

8. The Yogin whose self is satisfied with knowledge, and wisdom, who remains unshaken, who has conquered the senses, he is said to be a saint, — for whom a lump of earth, a stone and gold are equal.

9. He is esteemed, who is of the same mind to the good-hearted, friends, foes, the indifferent, the neutral, the hateful, relatives, the righteous, and the unrighteous.

Directions for the practice of Yoga

10. Let the Yogin try constantly to keep the mind steady, remaining in seclusion, alone, with the mind and body controlled, free from desire, and having no possessions.

11. Having in a cleanly spot established a firm seat, neither too high nor too low, with cloth, skin, and kusa grass thereon;

12. Making the mind one-pointed, with the actions of the mind and the senses controlled, let him, seated there on the seat, practice Yoga for the purification of the self.

13. Holding erect and still the body, head, and neck, firm, gazing on the tip of his nose, without looking around;

14. Serene-minded, fearless, firm in the vow of godly life,

having restrained the mind, thinking on Me, and balanced, let him sit, looking up to Me as the Supreme.

15. Thus always keeping the mind balanced, the Yogin, with the mind controlled, attains to the Peace abiding in Me, which culminates in Nirvana (moksha)

16. Yoga is not possible for him who eats too much, nor for him who does not eat at all, nor for him who is addicted to too much sleep, nor for him who is (ever) wakeful.

17. To him whose food and recreation are moderate, whose exertion in actions is moderate, whose sleep and waking are moderate, to him accrues Yoga which is destructive of pain.

Consummation

18. When the well-restrained thought is established in the Self only, without longing for any of the objects of desire, then he is said to be a Saint.

19. 'As a lamp in a sheltered spot does not flicker,' — this has been thought as the simile of a Yogin of subdued thought, practicing Yoga in the Self.

20. When thought is quiescent, restrained by the practice of Yoga; when, seeing the Self by the self, he is satisfied in his own Self.

21. When he knows that Infinite Joy which, transcending the senses, can be grasped by reason; when, steady (in the Self), he moves never from the Reality.

22. When, having obtained it, he thinks no other acquisition superior to it; when, therein established, he is not moved even by a great pain.

23. This severance from union with pain, be it known, is

called union (Yoga). That Yoga must be practiced with determination and with undepressed heart.

Further directions concerning the practice of Yoga

24. Abandoning without reserve all fancy-born desires, well-restraining all the senses from all quarters by the mind.

25. Little by little let him withdraw, by reason (buddhi) held in firmness; keeping the mind established in the Self, let him not think of anything.

26. By whatever cause the wavering and un- steady mind wanders away, from that let him restrain it and bring it back direct under the control of the Self.

The effect of Dhyana-Yoga

27. Supreme Bliss verily comes to this Yogin, whose mind is quite tranquil, whose passion is quieted, who has become Brahman, who is blemishless.

28. Thus always keeping the self steadfast, the Yogin, freed from sins, attains with ease to the infinite bliss of contact with the (Supreme) Brahman.

29. The Self abiding in all beings, and all beings (abiding) in the Self, sees he whose self has been made steadfast by Yoga, who everywhere sees the same.

30. He who sees Me everywhere and sees everything in Me, to him I vanish not, nor to Me does he vanish.

31. Whoso, intent on unity, worships Me who abide in all beings, that Yogin dwells in Me, whatever his mode of life.

32. Whoso, by comparison with himself, sees the same everywhere, Arjuna, be it pleasure or pain, he is deemed the highest Yogin.

Practice and indifference are the surest means to Yoga

Arjuna said:

33. This Yoga in equanimity, taught by you, Krishna, — I see not its steady continuance, because of the restlessness (of the mind).

34. The mind verily, is, restless, turbulent, strong, and obstinate. Thereof the restraint I deem quite as difficult as that of the wind.

The Blessed Lord said:

35. Doubtless, the mind is hard to restrain and restless; but by practice and by indifference it may be restrained.

36. Yoga, methinks, is hard to attain for a man of uncontrolled self; but by him who (often) strives, self-controlled, it can be acquired by (proper) means.

Failures in Yoga and the after-career

Arjuna said:

37. He who strives not, but who is possessed of faith, whose mind wanders away from Yoga, — having failed to attain perfection in Yoga, what end does he meet?

38. Having failed in both, does he not perish like a riven cloud, supportless and perplexed in the path to Brahman?

39. This doubt of mine, Krishna, do dispel completely; for none other than you can possibly destroy this doubt.

The Blessed Lord said:

40. Arjuna, neither in this world nor in the next is there destruction for him; none who does good ever comes to grief.

41. Having attained to the worlds of the righteous, and having dwelt there for eternal years, he who failed in Yoga is reborn in a house of the pure and wealthy.

42. Else, he is born in a family of wise Yogins only. This, verily, a birth like this, is very hard to obtain in this world.

43. There he gains touch with the knowledge that was acquired in the former body and strives more than before for perfection.

44. By that very former practice is he borne on, though unwilling. Even he who merely wishes to know of Yoga rises superior to the Word-Brahman.

The best of the Yogins

45. Verily, a Yogin who strives with assiduity, purified from sins and perfected in the course of many births, then reaches the Supreme Goal.

46. A Yogin is deemed superior to men of austerity, and superior to even men of knowledge; he is also superior to men of action; therefore, be a Yogin.

47. Of all Yogins, whoso, full of faith, worships Me with his inner self abiding in Me, he is deemed by Me as most devout.

7 – VIJNANA-YOGA (Yoga of Knowledge and Judgement)

Realization of the Lord by meditation

The Blessed Lord said:

1. With the mind intent on Me, Arjuna, practicing Yoga, and finding refuge in Me, how in full without doubt you shall know Me.

2. I shall fully teach you this knowledge combined with experience, which being known, nothing more besides here remains to be known.

3. Among thousands of men, one perchance strives for perfection; even among those who strive and are perfect, only one perchance knows me in truth.

Evolution of the Universe out of Divine Prakriti

4. Earth, water, fire, air, ether, thought (Manas) and reason (Buddhi), egoism (Ahamkara) – thus is My Prakriti divided eightfold.

5. This is the inferior (Prakriti); but as distinct from this

know My superior Prakriti, the very life by which this universe is upheld.

6. Know that all beings have their birth in these. So, I am the source and dissolution of the whole universe.

7. There is naught else higher than I, Arjuna; in Me all this is woven as clusters of gems on a string.

The divine principle penetrating the Universe

8. I am the sapidity in water. I am the light in the moon and the sun. I am the syllabic Om in all the Vedas, sound in ether, humanity in men.

9. And I am the agreeable odor in the earth and the brilliance in the fire, the vitality in all beings, and I am the austerity in ascetics.

10. Know Me as the eternal seed of all beings; I am the intelligence of the intelligent, the bravery of the brave.

11. And of the energetic am I the energy devoid of passion and attachment; and in (all) beings I am the desire unopposed to dharma.

12. And whatever beings are of Sattva or of Rajas or of Tamas, know them to proceed from Me; still, I am not in them, they are in me.

Maya: How to overcome it

13. Deluded by these three (sorts of) things composed of gunas, all this world knows not Me as distinct from them and immutable.

14. Verily this Divine Illusion of Mine, made up of gunas, is hard to surmount. Whoever seek Me alone, they cross over this Illusion.

15. Not Me do the evil-doers seek, the deluded, the vilest of men, deprived of wisdom by Illusion, following the ways of the Demons.

Four classes of devotees

16. Four kinds of virtuous men worship Me, Arjuna, — the distressed, the seeker of knowledge, the seeker of wealth, and the wise man.

17. Of them the wise man, ever steadfast and devoted to the One, excels; for, excessively dear am I to the wise, and he is dear to Me.

18. Noble indeed are all those; but the wise man, I deem, is the very Self; for, steadfast in mind, he resorts to Me alone as the unsurpassed goal.

19. At the end of many births, the man of wisdom comes to Me, (realizing) that Vasudeva is the all; he is the noble-souled (Mahatman), very hard to find.

The ignorant worship inferior Gods

20. Those whose wisdom has been led away by this or that desire resort to other Gods, engaged in this or that rite, constrained by their own nature.

21. Whatever devotee seeks to worship with faith what form soever, that same faith of his I make unflinching.

22. Possessed of that faith he engages in the worship of that (form); thence he obtains his desires, these being indeed ordained by Me.

23. That result indeed is finite, (which accrues) to those men of small intellect. Worshippers of Gods (Devatas) go to Gods (Devatas); My devotees come unto Me.

24. The foolish regard Me as the unmanifested coming into manifestation, knowing not My higher, immutable, unsurpassed nature.

25. I am not manifest to all, veiled (as I am) by Yoga-Maya. This deluded world knows not Me, unborn and imperishable.

26. I know the past and the present and the future beings, but Me nobody knows.

The root of ignorance

27. From the delusion of pairs caused by desire and aversion, Arjuna, all beings are subject to illusion at birth.

Divine worship leads to realization

28. Those mortals of pure deeds whose sin has come to an end, who are freed from the delusion of pairs, they worship Me with a firm resolve.

29. Whoever resorting to Me strive for liberation from decay and death, they realize in full that Brahman, the individual Self, and all action.

30. Those who realize Me in the Adhibhuta (physical region), in the Adhidaiva (the divine region) and in the Adhiyajwa (region of Sacrifice), realise Me even at the time of departure, steadfast in mind.

8 – ABHYASA-YOGA (Yoga of the Imperishable Brahman)

The seven things to be realized by meditation

Arjuna said:

1 — 2. What is that Brahman? What about the Individual Self (Adhyatma)? What is action (Karma)? And what is declared to be the physical region (Adhibhuta)? And what is the divine region (Adhidaiva) said to be? And how and who is Adhiyajna (the Entity concerned with Sacrifice) here in this body? and how at the time of death are you to be known by the self-controlled?

The Blessed Lord said:

3. Brahman is the Imperishable (Akshara), the Supreme. The Ego is said to be the Individual Self (Adhyatma, He who dwells in the body). The offering which causes the origin of physical beings is called action (Karma).

4. The physical region (Adhibiita) is the perishable existence, and Purusha or the Soul is the divine region (Adhidaivata). The Adhiyaj;ia (Entity concerned with Sacrifice) is Myself,

here in the body.

5. And whoso, at the time of death, thinking of Me alone, leaves the body and goes forth, he reaches My being; there is no doubt in this.

Constant meditation of the Divine is necessary

6. Of whatever Being thinking at the end a man leaves the body. Him alone, Arjuna, reaches he by whom the thought of that Being has been constantly dwelt upon.

7. Therefore at all times meditate on Me and fight with mind and reason fixed on Me you shall shalt doubtless come to Me alone.

The Divine Being to be meditated upon

8. Meditating with the mind engaged in the Yoga of constant practice, not passing over to anything else, one goes to the Supreme Purusha.

9 — 10. Whoso meditates on the Sage, the Ancient, the Ruler, smaller than an atom, the Dispenser of all, of unthinkable nature, glorious like the Sun, beyond the darkness, (whoso meditates on such a Being) at the time of death, with a steady mind endued with devotion and strength of Yoga, well fixing the life-breath betwixt the eye-brows, he reaches that Supreme Purusha.

Meditation of the Divine in the Pranava

11. That Imperishable Goal which the knowers of the Veda declare, which the self-controlled and the passion-free enter, which desiring they load the godly life, — That Goal will I declare to you with brevity.

12-13. Having closed all the gates, having con- fined mind in the heart, having fixed his life-breath in the head, engaged in firm Yoga, uttering Brahman, the one-syllabled 'Om,' thinking of Me, who- so departs, leaving the body, he reaches the Supreme Goal.

No re-birth on attaining to the Divine Bring

14. Whoso constantly thinks of Me and long, to him I am easily accessible to the ever-devout Yogin.

15. Having attained to Me, they do not again attain birth, which is the seat of pain and is not eternal, they having reached highest perfection.

16. (All) worlds including the world of Brahma are subject to returning again, Arjuna; but on reaching Me there is no rebirth.

The day and night of Brahma

17. Those people who know day and night — know that the day of Brahma is a thousand yugas long and the night is a thousand yugas long.

18. From the Unmanifested all the manifestations proceed at the coming on of day; at the coming of of night they dissolve there only, in what is called the Unmanifested.

19. This same multitude of beings, having come into being again and again, is dissolved at the coming of night, not of their will and comes forth at the coming on of day.

Th highest goal – how reached

20. But that other eternal Unmanifested Being, distinct from this Unmanifested (Avyakta), — He does not perish when all creatures perish.

21. What is called the Unmanifested and the Imperishable, That, they say, is the highest goal; which having reached none return. That is My highest place.

22. Now, that Highest Purusha, within Whom all beings dwell, by Whom all this is pervaded, is attainable by exclusive devotion.

The Paths of Light and Darkness

23. Now, in what time departing, Yogins go to return not, as also to return, that time will I tell you.

24. Fire, light, daytime, the bright fortnight, the six months of the northern solstice, — then departing, men who know Brahman reach Brahman.

25. Smoke, night-time, and the dark fortnight, the six months of the southern solstice, — attaining by these to the lunar light, the Yogin returns.

26. These bright and dark Paths of the world are verily deemed eternal; by the one a man goes to return not, by the other he returns.

27. Knowing these paths no Yogin is deluded; wherefore at all times be stead- fast in Yoga, Arjuna.

Excellence in Yoga

28. Whatever fruit of merit is declared to accrue from the Vedas, sacrifices, austerities, and gifts, — beyond all this goes the Yogin on knowing this; and he attains to the Supreme Primeval Abode.

9 – RAJA YOGA (Royal Yoga)

Brahma-Jnana is the best religion

The Blessed Lord said:

1. To you who do not cavil, I shall now declare this, the greatest secret, knowledge combined with experience, which having known you shall be liberated from evil.

2. The Sovereign Science, the Sovereign Secret, the Supreme Purifier is this; immediately comprehensible, unopposed to Dharma, very easy to perform, imperishable.

3. Persons having no faith in this Dharma, Arjuna, without reaching Me, remain verily in the path of the mortal world.

All beings rest in the Lord

4. By Me all this world is pervaded, My form unmanifested. All beings dwell in Me; and I do not dwell in them.

5. Nor do those beings dwell in Me; behold My Divine Yoga! Sustaining all beings, but not dwelling in them, is My Self, the cause of beings.

6. As the mighty wind moving everywhere rests ever in the

akasa, so, know thou, do all beings, rest in Me.

The Lord is the source and the end of all beings

7. All beings go into My Prakriti at the end of a kalpa. I send them forth again at the beginning of (the next) kalpa. Pvakviti.

8. Resorting to My Prakriti, I again and again send forth this whole multitude of beings, powerless under the control of the Prakriti.

The Lord is not bound by His acts

9. Nor do these acts bind Me, remaining like one unconcerned, unattached to those acts.

10. By Me presiding, Prakriti produces the moving and the unmoving; because of this the world revolves.

The life of the impious

11. Fools disregard Me clad in human form, not knowing My higher being as the Great Lord of beings.

12. Of vain hopes, of vain actions, of vain knowledge, devoid of discrimination, partaking only of the delusive nature of Rakshasas and Asuras.

The ways of the faithful devotees

13. The Mahatmans partaking of the nature of the Devas, worship Me with mind turned to no other, knowing (Me) as the imperishable source of all beings.

14. Always talking of Me, strenuous, firm in vows, and reverent, they worship Me with love, always devout.

15. Worshipping by the wisdom-sacrifice, others adore Me, the All-faced, in various ways, as One, as different.

All worship goes to the Lord

16. I am kratu, I am yajna, I am svadha, I am aushadha, I am mantra, Myself the butter, I am fire, I the act of offering.

17. I am the father of this world, the mother, the dispenser, and grandsire; I am the knowable, the purifier, the syllable ' Om,' and also the Rik, the Saman, and the Yajus also.

18. I am the Goal, the Sustainer, the Lord, the Witness, the Abode, the Shelter and the Friend, the Origin, Dissolution and Stay; the Treasure-house, the Seed imperishable.

19. I give heat, I hold back and send forth rain, I am the immortality as well as death, existence and non-existence.

The fruits of interested acts of Vedic ritual

20. Men of the three Vedas, the soma-drinkers, purified from sin, worshipping Me by sacrifices, pray for the goal of heaven; they reach the holy world of the Lord of the Gods and enjoy in heaven the heavenly pleasures of the Gods.

21. They, having enjoyed that spacious world of Svarga, their merit (punya) exhausted, enter the world of the mortals; thus following the Dharma of the Triad, desiring (objects of) desires, they attain to the state of going and returning.

The Supreme watching over His devotees' interest

22. Those men who, meditating on Me as non-separate, worship Me all around, — to them who are ever devout, I secure gain and safety.

Other devotees do but worship the Supreme in ignorance

23. Even those who, devoted to other Gods, worship Them with faith, worship Myself in ignorance.

24. I am indeed the Enjoyer, as also the Lord, of all

sacrifices; but they do not know Me in truth; whence they fail.

25. Votaries of the Gods go to the Gods; to the Pitris go the votaries of the Pitris; to the Bhutas go the worshippers of the Bhutas; My worshippers come to Myself.

Facility in Devotion to the Supreme

26. When one offers to Me with devotion a leaf, a flower, a fruit, water, — that I eat, offered with devotion by the pure-minded.

27. Whatever you do, whatever you eat, whatever you sacrifice, whatever you give, in whatever austerity you engage, do it as an offering to Me.

28. Thus you shall be liberated from the bonds of actions which are productive of good and evil results; equipped in mind with the Yoga of renunciation, and liberated, you shall come to Me.

The impartiality of the Supreme

29. The same I am to all beings; to Me there is none hateful or dear; but whoso worship Me with devotion, they are in Me, and I am also in them.

Even the low-born attain by Devotion

30. If one of even very evil life worships Me, resorting to none else, he must indeed be deemed righteous, for he is rightly resolved.

31. Soon he becomes righteous and attains eternal peace; I proclaim that My devotee never perishes.

32. For, finding refuge in Me, they also who may be of a sinful birth — women, vaisyas as well as siidras, — even they attain to the Supreme Goal.

The Yoga of Devotion

33. How much more than the holy brahmanas and devoted royal saints. Having reached this transient joyless world, worship Me.

34. Fix your mind on Me, be devoted to Me, sacrifice to Me, bow down to Me. Thus steadied, with Me as your Supreme Goal, you shall reach Myself, the Self.

10 - DIVINE MANIFESTATIONS (Yoga of Divine Manifestations)

The Lord is the source of all manifestations

The Blessed Lord said:

1. Again, Arjuna, listen to My Supreme word, which I, from a desire for your well-being, shall speak to you who are delighted.

2. Neither the hosts of the Gods nor the Great Rishis know my origin; for I am the source of all the Gods and the Great Rishis.

3. He who knows Me as unborn and beginningless, as the great Lord of the worlds, he among mortals is undeluded, he is liberated from all sins.

4-5. Intelligence, wisdom, non-illusion, patience, truth, self-restraint, calmness, pleasure, pain, birth, death, fear, and security; innocence, equanimity, contentment, austerity, beneficence, fame, shame; (these) different kinds of dispositions of beings arise from Me alone.

6. The seven Great Rishis as well as the four ancient Manus, with their being in Me, were born of mind; and theirs are these creatures in the world.

Knowledge of the Lord's Glory conduces to Yoga

7. He who knows in truth this glory and power of Mine is endowed with unshaken Yoga; there is no doubt of it.

8. I am the source of all; from Me everything evolves; thus, thinking the wise worship Me, endowed with contemplation.

9. With their thought on Me, with their life absorbed in Mc, instructing each other, and ever speaking of Me, they are content and delighted.

The Lord endows His devotees with wisdom

10. To these, ever devout, worshipping Me with love, I give that devotion of knowledge by which they come to Me.

11. Out of mere compassion for them, I, abiding in their self, destroy the darkness born of ignorance, by the luminous lamp of wisdom.

Arjuna said:

12-13. The Supreme Brahman, the Supreme Light, the Supreme Purifier you are. All the Rishis declare you as Eternal, Divine Pursha, the Primal God, Unborn, Omnipresent; so said the divine sage Narada, as also Asita, Devala, and Vyasa; and you yourself also say (so) to me.

14. I believe to be true all this which you have said to me; for neither the Gods nor the Danavas, O Lord, know your manifestation.

15. You know yourself as the Self, Purusha Supreme, Source of beings, Lord of beings, God of Gods, Ruler of the world.

16. You should not indeed tell, without reserve, of your divine Glories, by which Glories you remain pervading all these worlds.

17. How shall I, ever meditating, know you; in what several things are you to be thought of by Me?

18. Tell me again in detail, Krishna, of your power and Glory, for there is no satiety for me in hearing the immortal.

The Lord's enumeration of His manifestations

The Blessed Lord said:

19. Now will I tell you of My heavenly Glories, in their prominence, Arjuna; there is no limit to My extent.

20. I am the Self seated in the heart of all beings; I am the beginning and the middle, as also the end, of all beings.

21. Of the Adityas I am Vishnu; of the radiances, the resplendent Sun; I am Marichi of the Maruts; of the asterisms, the Moon.

22. Of the Vedas I am the Sama-Veda, I am Vasava of the Gods, and of the senses I am the mind, I am the intelligence in living beings.

23. And of the Rudras I am Sankara, of the Yakshas and Rakshasas the Lord of wealth, and of the Vasus I am Agni, of the mountains I am the Meru.

24. And of the household priests of kings know Me the chief one, Brihaspati; of generals I am Skanda, of lakes I am the Ocean.

25. Of the Great Rishis I am Bhrigu; of words I am the one syllable ' Om;' of offerings I am the offering of Japa (silent repetition), of unmoving things the Himalaya.

26. Of all trees (I am) the Asvattha, and Narada of divine Rishis, Chitraratha of Gandharvas, the Sage Kapila of the Saints (Siddhas).

27. Know Me among horses as Uchchais- sravas, born of Amrita, of lordly elephants the Airavata, and of men the king.

28. Of weapons I am the thunderbolt, of cows I am the Kamadhuk, I am the progenitor Kandarpa, of serpents I am Vasnki.

29. And Ananta of snakes I am, I am Varuna of water-beings, and Aryaman of Pitris I am, I am Yama of controllers.

30. And Prahlada am I of Diti's progeny, of reckoners I am Time, and of beasts I am the lord of beasts, and Vainateya of birds.

31. Of purifiers I am the wind, Rama of warriors am I, of fishes I am the shark, of streams I am the Ganges.

32. Of creations I am the beginning and the middle and also the end; of all knowledges I am the knowledge of the Self, and Vada of disputants.

33- Of letters the letter 'A' am I, and dvandva of all compounds; I am, verily, the inexhaustible Time; I am the All-faced Dispenser.

34. And I am all-seizing Death, and the prosperity of those who are to be prosperous; of the feminine (I am) Fame, Fortune and Speech, Memory, Intelligence, Constancy, Endurance.

35. Of Samans also I am the Brihat-Saman, of metres Gayatri

am I, of months I am Margasirsha, of seasons the flowery season.

36. I am the gambling of the fraudulent, I am the splendor of the splendid, I am victory, I am effort, I am the goodness of the good.

37. Of the Vrishnis I am Vasudeva, of the Pandavas I am Dhananjaya, and of the saints I am Vyasa, of the sages I am Usanas the sage.

38, Of punishers I am the scepter, of those who seek to conquer I am the polity, and things secret I am also silence, the knowledge of knowers am I.

39. And what is the seed of all beings, that also am I, Arjuna. There is no being, whether moving or unmoving that can exist without me.

40. There is no end of My heavenly Glories, but the details of My glory have been declared only by the way of instance.

Divine Flory described in brief

41. Whatever being is glorious, prosperous, or strong, that know you to be a manifestation of a part of My Splendor.

42. But, of what avail to you is this vast thing being known, Arjuna? I stand sustaining this whole world by one part (of Myself).

11 - THE UNIVERSAL FORM (Yoga of the Cosmic Vision)

Arjuna's prayer for a vision of the Universal Form

Arjuna said:

1. By that speech which has been delivered by you for my benefit, — that highest secret, which is called Adhyatma, — this, my delusion, is gone.

2. The origin and the dissolution of beings, verily, have been heard by me in detail from you, Krishna, as also your inexhaustible greatness.

3. So it is, as you, the Supreme Lord, has declared yourself to be. (Still) I desire to see your form as Isvara.

4. If you think it possible for me to see it, then show me your Eternal Self.

Arjuna endowed with heavenly sight to see the Universal Form

The Blessed Lord said:

5. See My heavenly forms, by hundreds and thousands, of different sorts, and of various colors and shapes.

6 Behold the Adityas, the Vasus, the Rudras, the Asvins, and also the Maruts; behold many marvels never seen before, Arjuna.

7. Now behold here in My body the whole world established in one, — including the moving and the unmoving — and whatever else you desire to see.

8. You cannot able to see Me with your eyes alone; I give you a divine eye; behold My lordly Yoga.

The Lord's manifestation of the Universal Form

Sanjaya said:

9. Having thus spoken, King, then, Krishna showed to Arjuna the Supreme Form as Isvara.

10. Containing many mouths and eyes, possessed of many wondrous sights, of many heavenly ornaments, of many heavenly weapons held up; Such a form He showed.

11. Wearing heavenly garlands and vestures, anointed with heavenly unguents, all-wonderful, resplendent, boundless, with faces on all sides.

12. If the splendor of a thousand suns were ever to present itself at once in the sky, that would be like the splendor of that Mighty Being.

13. There, in the body of the God of Gods, Arjuna then beheld the whole world established in one, and separated into many groups.

14. Then he, Arjuna, filled with amazement, with his hair standing on end, bowed down with his head, and, with joined

palms, thus addressed the God.

Arjuna said:

15. I see all the Gods, O God, in your body, as also hosts of various classes of beings: Brahma, the Lord, seated on the lotus-seat, and all Rishis and heavenly serpents.

16. I see you of boundless form on every side with multitudinous arms, stomachs, mouths, and eyes; neither end nor the middle nor the beginning do I see.

17. I see you with diadem, club, and discus; a mass of splendor shining everywhere, very hard to look at, all around blazing like burning fire and sun, and immeasurable.

Vishnu is one with the Unconditioned

18. You are the Imperishable, the Supreme Being worthy to be known. You are the great Abode of this Universe; You are the undying Guardian of the Eternal Dharma, You are the ancient Purusha.

The Universal Form

19. I see you without beginning, middle or end, infinite in power, of manifold arms; the sun and the moon being your eyes, the burning fire your face; heating the whole Universe with your radiance.

20. This space between heaven and earth and all the quarters are filled by you alone. Having seen this. Your marvelous and awful form, the three worlds are trembling in your Universal Form.

21. Into you enter these hosts of Suras; some extol you in fear with joined palms; "May it be well!"thus saying, bands of great Rishis and Siddhas praise you with hymns complete.

The wonderfulness of the Universal Form

22. The Rudras, Adityas, Vasus, and Sadhyas, Visvas and Asvins, Maruts and Ushmapas, hosts of Gandharvas, Yakshas, Asuras, and Siddhas, — they are all looking at you, all quite astonished.

23. Having seen your immeasurable Form, possessed of many mouths and eyes, of many arms and thighs and feet, and of many stomachs, and fearful with many tusks, the worlds are terrified, and I also.

24. On seeing your form touching the sky, blazing in many colors, with mouths wide open, with large fiery eyes, I am terrified at heart and find no courage nor peace.

25. Having seen your mouths which are fearful with tusks and resemble Time's Fires, I know not the four quarters, nor do I find peace.

Arjuna's vision of the defeat of the enemy

26 — 27. And all these sons of Dhntarashira, with hosts of princes, Bhishma, Drona and that son (Karna) of a charioteer, with the warrior chiefs of ours, enter hurrying into your mouth, terrible with tusks and fearful to behold. Some are found sticking in the gaps betwixt the teeth with their heads crushed to powder.

28. As many torrents of rivers flow direct towards the sea, so do these heroes in the world of men enter your flaming mouths.

29. As moths hurriedly rush into a blazing fire for destruction, just so do these creatures also hurriedly rush into your mouths for destruction.

The splendor of the Universal Form

30. You are devouring all worlds on every side with your flaming mouths, filling the whole world with flames. Your fierce rays are blazing forth.

31. Tell me who are you, so fierce in form. I bow to you; have mercy. I desire to know you, the Original Being. I know not indeed your doing.

The Lord's advent for destruction of worlds

The Blessed Lord said:

32. I am the mighty world-destroying Time, now engaged in destroying the worlds. Even without you, none of the warriors arrayed in hostile armies shall live.

33. Therefore arise and obtain fame. Conquer the enemies and enjoy the unrivalled dominion. By Myself have they been already slain, be you a mere instrument, Arjuna.

34. Drona and Bhishma, Jayadratha, Kama and other brave warriors, — these, killed by Me, you should also kill; fear not, fight, you shall conquer the enemies.

Arjuna's adoration of the Universal Form

Sanjaya said:

35. Having heard that speech of Arjuna, with joined palms, trembling, prostrating himself, again addressed Krishna, stammering, bowing down, overwhelmed with fear.

Arjuna said:

36. It is meet, Krishna, that the world is delighted and rejoices by your praise; Rakshasas fly in fear to all quarters, and all hosts of Siddhas bow to you.

37. And how should they not bow to you, Greater (than all else), the Primal Cause even of Brahma. You are the Imperishable, the Being and the non-Being, That which is the Supreme.

38. You are the Primal God, the Ancient Purusha; Then are the Supreme Abode of all this. You are the Knower and the Knowable and the Supreme Abode. By you is all pervaded.

39. You are Vayu, Yama, Agni, Varuna, the Moon, Prajapati, and the Great Grandfather. Hail! Hail to you! A thousand times, and again and again hail!

40. Hail to you before and behind! Hail to you on every side! You are infinite in power and infinite in daring, pervading all.

Arjuna's prayer for the Lord's forgiveness

41-42. Whatever was rashly said by me from carelessness or love, addressing you as "Krishna, friend"looking on you merely as a friend, ignorant of this your greatness, — in whatever way I may have insulted you for fun while at play, on bed, in an assembly, or at meals, when alone, or in company — that I implore you to forgive me.

43. You are the Father of this world, moving and unmoving. You are to be adored by this (world). You are the Greatest Guru; (for) your equal exists not; whence another, superior to you, in the three worlds?

44. Therefore, bowing down, prostrating my body, I implore you, adorable Lord, to forgive. It is me you should bear with me as the father with the son, as friend with friend, as the lover with the beloved.

Arjuna's prayer for the Lord's resumption of His usual form

45. I am delighted, having seen what was unseen before; and (yet) my mind is confounded with fear. Show me that form only; have mercy.

46. I wish to see you as before, crowned, possessed of the club, with the discus in the hand, in your former form only, having four arms.

The Lord resumes His usual form

The Blessed Lord said:

47. By Me, gracious to you, Arjuna, this Supreme Form has been shown, — by my sovereign power — full of splendor, the All, the Boundless, the Original Form of Mine, never before seen by any other than yourself.

48. Not by study of the Vedas and of the sacrifices, nor by gifts, nor by rituals, nor by severe austerities, can I be seen in this Form in the world of man by any other than yourself.

49. Be not afraid nor bewildered on seeing such a terrible form of Mine as this; free from fear and cheerful at heart, do you again see this My former form.

Sanjaya said:

50. Having thus spoken to Arjuna, Krishna again showed His own form; and the Mighty Being, becoming gentle in form, consoled him who was terrified.

Arjuna said:

51. Having seen this, your gentle human form, Krishna, now I have grown serene, and returned to my nature.

Devotion as the sole means to the realization of the Universal Form

The Blessed Lord said:

52. Very hard to see is this Form of Mine which you have seen; even the Devas ever long to behold this form.

53. Not by Vedas, nor by austerity, nor by gifts, nor by sacrifice, can I be seen in this Form as you have seen Me.

54. But by undistracted devotion can I, of this Form, be known and seen in reality, and entered into.

55. He who does works for Me, who looks on Me as the Supreme, who is devoted to Me, who is free from attachment, who is without hatred for any being, he comes to Me.

12 – BHAKTI-YOGA (Yoga of Devotion)

Who are superior - the worshipers of Isvara, or Akshara?

Arjuna said:

1. Those devotees who contemplate you, and those also who contemplate the Imperishable, the Unmanifest, — which of them are better versed in Yoga?

The Blessed Lord said:

2. Those who, fixing their thought on Me, contemplate Me, always devout, endued with supreme faith, those are the best.

Worshipers of Akshara

3-4. Those who ever contemplate the Imperishable, the Indefinable, the Unmanifest, the Omnipresent and the Unthinkable, the Unchangeable, the Immutable, the Eternal, — having restrained all the senses, always equanimous, intent on the welfare of all beings - they reach Myself.

5. Greater is their trouble whose thoughts are set on the Unmanifest; for, the Goal, the Unmanifest, is very hard for

the embodied to reach.

6-7. But those who worship Me, renouncing all actions in Me, regarding Me Supreme, meditating on Me with exclusive devotion (yoga); for them whose thought is fixed on Me, I become the deliverer out of the ocean of the mortal samsara.

8. Fix your mind in Me exclusively apply your reason to Me. You shall no doubt live in Me alone hereafter.

Abhyasa-Yoga

9. If you are unable to fix your thought steadily on Me, then by yoga of constant practice you shall reach Me, Arjuna.

Service of the Lord

10. (If) you are not able to practice either, then be your intent on (doing) actions for My sake. Even doing actions for My sake, you shall attain perfection.

Abandonment of the fruits of actions

11. If you are unable to do even this, then take refuge in devotion to Me, abandon the fruits of all actions, self-controlled.

12. Better indeed is knowledge than practice; than knowledge is meditation more esteemed; than meditation the abandonment of the fruits of actions; on abandonment, Peace follows immediately.

The life of the Akshara-upasakas

13-14. He who hates no single being, who is friendly and compassionate to all, who is free from attachment and egoism, to whom pain and pleasure are equal, who is enduring, ever content and balanced in mind, self-controlled, and possessed of firm conviction, whose thought and reason are directed to Me, he who is (thus) devoted to

Me is dear to Me.

15. He by whom the world is not afflicted and who is not afflicted by the world, who is free from joy, envy, fear, and sorrow, he is dear to Me.

16. He who is free from wants, who is pure, clever, unconcerned, untroubled, renouncing all undertakings, he who is (thus) devoted to Me is dear to me.

17. He who neither rejoices, nor hates, nor grieves, nor desires, renouncing good and evil, he who is full of devotion is dear to me.

18- 19. He who is the same to foe and friend, and also in honor and dishonor: who is the same in cold and heat, in pleasure and pain: who is free from attachment; to whom censure and praise are equal; who is silent, content with anything, homeless, steady-minded, full of devotion; that man is dear to Me.

20. They, verily, who follow this immortal Law described above, endued with faith, looking up to Me as the Supreme, and devoted, they are exceeding dear to Me.

13 - MATTER AND SPIRIT (The Field and its Knower)

The main subject of the discourse

The Blessed Lord said:

1. This, the body, Arjuna , is called Kshetra (matter); him who knows it, they who know of them call Kshetrajna.

Identity of the soul with the Lord

2. And also know Me as Kshetrajna (spirit) in all Kshetras. The knowledge of Kshetra and Kshetrajna is deemed by Me as the knowledge

Summary of the doctrine

3. And what that Kshetra (matter) is, and of what nature, and what its changes; and whence is what; and who He is and what His powers; this hear briefly from Me.

The doctrine extolled

4. Sung by sages, in many ways and distinctly, in various hymns, as also in the suggestive words about Brahman, full of reasoning and decisive.

Matter in all its forms

5. The Great Elements, Egoism, Reason, as also the Unmanifested, the ten senses and one, and the five objects of the senses;

6. Desire, hatred, pleasure, pain, the aggregate, intelligence, courage; — the Kshetra has been thus briefly described with its modifications.

Virtues conductive to self-knowledge

7. Humility, modesty, innocence, patience, up- rightness, service of the teacher, purity, steadfastness, self-control;

8. Absence of attachment for objects of the senses, and also absence of egoism; perception of evil in birth, death and old age, in sickness and pain;

9. Unattachment, absence of affection for son, wife, home and the like, and constant, equanimity on the attainment of the desirable and the undesirable;

10. Unflinching devotion to Me in Yoga of non- separation, resort to solitary places, distaste for the society of men;

11. Constancy in Self-knowledge, perception of the end of the knowledge of truth. This is declared to be knowledge, and what is opposed to it is ignorance.

Brahman, the knowable

12. That which has to be known I shall describe; knowing which one attains the Immortal. Beginningless is the Supreme Brahman. It is not said to be ' sat ' or ' asat.'

Brahman is the source of all activity

13. With hands and feet everywhere, with eyes and heads and mouths everywhere, with hearing everywhere. That exists enveloping all.

Brahman is unconditioned

14. Shining by the functions of all the senses, (yet) without the senses, unattached, yet supporting all; devoid of qualities; yet enjoying, qualities.

Brahman is all

15. Without and within (all) beings; the un- moving as also the moving. Because subtle, That is incomprehensible; and near and far away is That.

Brahman is the one Self in all

16. And undivided yet remaining divided as it were in beings; supporter of beings, too, is That, the Knowable; devouring, yet generating.

Brahman is the illuminator of all

17. The Light even of lights, That is said to be beyond darkness. Knowledge, the Knowable, the Goal of knowledge, (It) is implanted in the heart of everyone.

Seek the light through devotion

18. Thus the Kshetra, as well as knowledge and the Knowable, have been briefly set forth. My devotee, on knowing this, is fitted for My state.

Prakriti(matter) and Purusha(spirit) are eternal

19. Know that Prakriti (matter) as well as Purusha(spirit) are both beginningless; and know also that all forms and qualities are born of Prakriti.

Prakriti and Purusha as the cause of samsara

20. As the producer of the effect and the instruments, Prakriti is said to be the cause; as experiencing pleasure and pain, Purusha is said to be the cause.

Avidya and Kama are the cause of rebirths

21. Purusha, when seated in Prakriti, experiences the qualities born of Prakriti. Attachment to the qualities is the cause of his birth in good and evil wombs.

Self-knowledge removed the cause of samsara

22. Spectator and Permitter, Supporter, Enjoyer, the Great Lord, and spoken of as the Supreme Self, (is) the Purusha Supreme in this body.

23. He who thus knows Purusha and Prakriti together with qualities, whatever his conduct, he is not born again.

The four paths to self-knowledge

24. By meditation some behold the Self in the self by the self, others by Sankhya-Yoga, and others by Karma- Yoga.

25. Yet others, not knowing thus, worship, having heard from others; they, too, cross beyond death, adhering to what they heard.

Nothing exists outside the self

26. Whatever being is born, the unmoving or the moving, know thou, that to be owing to the union of Kshetra and Kshetrajna.

The one Self in all

27. He sees, who sees the Supreme Lord, remaining the same in all beings, the undying in the dying.

Knowledge of the one Self leads to moksha

28. Because he who sees the Lord, seated the same everywhere, destroys not the self by the self, therefore he reaches the Supreme Goal.

Prakriti acts, not the Self

29. He sees, who sees all actions performed by Prakriti alone and the Self not acting.

The Self is the source and the abode of all

30. When a man realizes the whole variety of beings as resting in the One, and as an evolution from that (One) alone, then he becomes Brahman.

The Self is unaffected by the fruits of acts

31. Having no beginning, having no qualities, this Supreme Self, imperishable, though dwelling in the body neither acts nor is tainted.

32. As the all-pervading akasa is, from its subtlety, never soiled, so the Self seated in the body everywhere is not soiled.

The Self illuminates all

33. As the one sun illumines all this world, so does the embodied One illumine all bodies.

The doctrine summed up

34. They who by the eye of wisdom perceive the distinction between Kshetra and Kshetrajna, and the dissolution of the Cause of beings, — they go to the Supreme.

14 - THE THREE GUNAS (Yoga of the Three Gunas)

Knowledge of the origins of the universe is necessary for Salvation

The Blessed Lord said:

1. I shall again declare that sublime knowledge, the best of all knowledges, which having learnt, all the sages have passed to high perfection from here.

2. They who, having resorted to this knowledge, have attained to unity with Me, are neither born in the creation, nor disturbed in the dissolution.

Evolution of the universe from the union of Spirit and Matter

3. My womb is the great Brahman; in that I place the germ; thence is the birth of all beings.

4. Whatever forms are produced in any wombs whatsoever, the Great Brahman is their womb, I the seed-giving Father.

The gunas bind the soul

5. Sattva, Rajas, Tamas, — these gunas born of Prakriti, bind fast in the body the embodied, the indestructible.

The nature and functions of the gunas

6. Of these, Sattva, which, from its stainlessness, is lucid and healthy, binds by attachment to happiness and by attachment to knowledge.

7. Know Rajas (to be) of the nature of passion, the source of thirst and attachment; it binds fast the embodied one by attachment to action.

8. But, know Tamas to be born of unwisdom, deluding all embodied beings; by heed- lessness, indolence and sloth, it binds fast.

9. Sattva attaches to happiness, Rajas to action, while Tamas, enshrouding wisdom, attaches, on the contrary, to heedlessness.

The mutual action of the gunas

10. Sattva arises, predominating over Rajas and Tamas; and Rajas, over Sattva and Tamas; so Tamas, over Sattva and Rajas.

How to know when a particular guna is predominant

11. When at every gate in this body there shoots up wisdom-light, then it may be known that Sattva is predominant.

12. Greed, activity, the undertaking of works, unrest, desire, — these arise when Rajas is predominant.

13. Darkness, heedlessness, inertness, and error, — these arise when Tamas is predominant.

Life after death as governed by the gunas

14. If the embodied one meets death when Sattva is predominant, then he attains to the spotless regions of the knowers of the Highest.

15. Meeting death in Rajas, he is born among those attached to action; and, dying in Tamas, he is born in the wombs of the irrational.

16. The fruit of good action, they say, is Sattvic and pure; while the fruit of Rajas is pain, and ignorance is the fruit of Tamas.

The functions of the gunas summer up

17. From Sattva arises wisdom, and greed from Rajas; heedlessness, error, and ignorance arise from Tamas.

18. Those who follow Sattva go upwards (as Gods); the Rajasic remain in the middle (as people); and the Tamasic go downwards (as animals).

Realization of the Self beyond the gunas leads to immortality

19. When the seer beholds not an agent other than the gunas and knows Him who is higher than the gunas, he attains to My being.

20. Having crossed beyond these three gunas, which are the source of the body, the embodied one is freed from birth, death, decay and pain, and attains the immortal.

The marks of a liberated soul

Arjuna said:

21. By what marks, Krishna, is he known who has crossed beyond those three gunas? What is his conduct, and how does he pass beyond those three gunas?

The Blessed Lord said:

22. Light and activity and delusion present, he hates not, nor longs for them absent.

The conduct in life of the Liberated one

23. He who, seated as a neutral, is not moved by gunas; who, thinking that gunas as act, is firm and moves not;

24. He to whom pain and pleasure are alike, who dwells in the Self, to whom a clod of earth and stone and gold are alike, to whom the dear and the undear are alike, who is a man of wisdom, to whom censure and praise are same;

25. The same in honor and disgrace, the same towards friends and enemies, abandoning all undertakings, — he is said to have crossed beyond the gunas.

26. And he who serves. Me with unfailing Devotion of Love, he, crossing beyond those three gunas, is fitted for becoming Brahman.

Unity of Atman

27. For I am the abode of Brahman, the Immortal and the Immutable, the Eternal Dharma, and the unfailing Bliss.

15 - THE SUPREME SPIRIT (Yoga of the Supreme Purusha)

The Tree of Samsara

The Blessed Lord said:

1. They speak of the indestructible Asvattha having its root above and branches below, whose leaves are the metres. He who knows it knows the Vedas.

2. Below and above are its branches spread, nourished by the gunas, sense-objects its buds; and below in the world of man stretch forth the roots ending in action.

Cut the Tree and seek the Goal

3. Its form is not perceived as such here, neither its end nor its origin nor its existence. Having cut asunder this firm rooted Asvattha with the strong sword of dispassion,

4. Then That Goal should be sought for, whither having gone none return. "I seek refuge in that Primeval Purusha whence streamed forth the Ancient Current."

The Path to the Goal

5. Free from pride and delusion, with the evil of attachment conquered, ever dwelling in the Self, their desires having completely turned away, liberated from the pairs of opposites known as pleasure and pain, the undeluded reach that Goal Eternal.

The Goal is the Lord's Glorious Being

6. That, the sun illumines not, nor the moon, nor fire; That is My Supreme Abode, to which having gone none return.

Jiva is a ray of the Lord

7. A ray of Myself, the eternal Jiva in the world of Jivas, attracts the senses, with manas the sixth, abiding in Prakriti.

How Jiva dwells in the body and departs from it

8. When the Lord acquires a body, and when He leaves it, He takes these and goes, as the wind takes scents from their seats.

9. The ear, the eye and the touch, the taste, and the smell, using these and the manas, he enjoys the sense-objects.

The Self is visible only to the eye of knowledge

10. Him who departs, stays, and enjoys, who is conjoined with gunas, the deluded perceive not; they see, who possess the eye of knowledge.

No self-knowledge without yoga

11. Those who strive, endued with Yoga, perceive Him dwelling in the self; though striving, those of unrefined self, devoid of wisdom, perceive Him not.

Immanence of the Lord (1) as the all-illumining Light of Consciousness

12. That light which residing in the sun illumines the whole

world, that which is in the moon and in the fire, that light know to be Mine.

(2) As the all-sustaining Life

13. Penetrating the earth I support all beings by (My) Energy; and having become the watery moon I nourish all herbs.

(3) As the Digestive Fire in all living organisms

14. Abiding in the body of living beings as Vaisvanara, associated with Prana and Apana, I digest the four-fold food.

(4) As the Self in the hearts of all

15. And I am seated in the hearts of all: from Me are memory, knowledge, as well as their loss; it is I who am to be known by all the Vedas, I am indeed the author of the Vedanta as well the knower of the Vedas.

The Lord beyond the perishable and the imperishable universe

16. There are these two beings in the world, the perishable and the imperishable: the perishable comprises all creatures; the immutable is called the imperishable.

17. But distinct is the Highest Spirit spoken of as the Supreme Self, the indestructible Lord who penetrates and sustains the three worlds.

18. Because I transcend the perishable and am even higher than the imperishable, therefore am I known in the world and in the Veda as 'Purushot- tama,' the Highest Spirit.

The Glory of Self-knowledge

19. He who, undeluded, thus knows Me, the Highest Spirit, he, knowing all, worships Me with his whole being.

20. Thus, this most Secret Science has been taught by Me; on knowing this, (a man) becomes wise and all his duties are accomplished.

16 - SPIRITUALITY AND MATERIALISM (Yoga of Divine and Undivine)

Spiritual disposition

The Blessed Lord said:

1. Fearlessness, purity of heart, steadfastness in knowledge and Yoga; alms-giving, self-restraint and worship, study of one's own (scriptures), austerity, uprightness;

2. Harmlessness, truth, absence of anger, renunciation, serenity, absence of calumny, com- passion to creatures, uncovetousness, gentleness, modesty, absence of fickleness;

3. Energy, forgiveness, fortitude, purity, absence of hatred, absence of pride; these belong to one born for a divine lot, Arjuna.

Materialistic disposition

4. Ostentation, arrogance and self-conceit, anger as also insolence, and ignorance, belong to one who is born for a demoniac lot.

5. The divine nature is deemed for liberation, the demoniac

for bondage. Grieve not, you are born for a divine lot.

The materialists

6. There are two creations of beings in this world, the divine and the demoniac. The divine has been described at length; hear from Me of the demoniac.

7. Neither action nor inaction do the demoniac men know; neither purity nor good conduct nor truth is found in them.

The materialist's view of the world

8. They say, "the universe is unreal, without a basis, without a Lord, born of mutual union, brought about by lust; what else?"

Men's life as guided by materialism

9. Holding this view, these ruined souls of small intellect, of fierce deeds, rise as the enemies of the world for its destruction.

10. Filled with insatiable desires, full of hypocrisy, pride and arrogance, holding unwholesome views through delusion, they work with unholy resolve;

11. Beset with immense cares ending only with death, sensual enjoyment their highest aim, assured that that is all;

12. Round by hundreds of bands of hope, given over to lust and wrath, they strive to secure by unjust means hordes of wealth for sensual enjoyment.

The materialists' aspirations

13. This today has been gained by me; this desire I shall attain; this is mine, and this wealth also shall be mine in future.

14. That enemy has been slain by me, and others also shall I

slay. I am a lord, I enjoy, I am successful, strong, and healthy.

15. I am rich and well-born. Who else is equal to me? I will sacrifice, I will give, I will rejoice. Thus deluded by unwisdom,

16. Bewildered by many a fancy, entangled in the snare of delusion, addicted to the gratification of lust, they fall into a foul hell.

The materialists' sacrificial rites

17. Self-honored, stubborn, filled with the pride and intoxication of wealth, they perform sacrifices in name with hypocrisy, without regard to ordinance.

The materialists' neglect of Divine Commandments

18. Given over to egotism, power, haughtiness, lust, and anger, these malicious people hate Me in their own and other's bodies.

The materialists' fall

19. These cruel haters, worst of men, I hurl these evil doers forever in the worlds into the wombs of the demons only.

20. Entering demoniac wombs, the deluded ones, in birth after birth, without ever reaching Me pass into a condition still lower than that.

The three gates of hell to be avoided

21. Triple is this, the gate to hell, destructive of the self: lust, wrath, and greed. Therefore, these three, one should abandon.

22. A man who is released from these, the three gates to darkness does good to the self, and thereby reaches the Supreme Goal.

Let the Law guide your life

23. He who, neglecting the scriptural ordinance, acts under the impulse of desire, attains not perfection, nor happiness, nor the Supreme Goal.

24. Therefore, the scripture is your authority in deciding as to what ought to be done and what ought not to be done. Now, you should know and perform your duty laid down in the scripture law.

17 – YOGA of the THREEFOLD FAITH

The ignorant, but faithful

Arjuna said:

1. Whoso worship, setting aside the ordinance of the scripture, endued with faith, — what faith is theirs? Is it Sattva, or Rajas, or Tamas?

The three kinds of Faith

The Blessed Lord said:

2. Threefold is that faith born of the individual nature of the embodied, — Sattvic, Rajasic, and Tamasic.

3. The faith of each is in accordance with his nature, Arjuna. The man is made up of his faith; as a man's faith is, so is he.

4. Sattvic men worship the Gods; Rajasic, the Yakshas and the Rakshasas; the others, — Tamasic men, — the Pretas and the hosts of Bhutas.

Men of Rajasic and Tamasic Faiths

5. Those men who practice terrific austerities not enjoined by the scripture, given to hypocrisy and egotism, endued with

the strength of lust and passion.

6. Weakening all the elements in the body — fools they are — and Me who dwell in the body within; know these to be of demoniac resolves.

Threefold Food, Worship, Austerity and Gift

7. The food also which is dear to each is threefold, as also worship, austerity, and gift. Do you hear of this, their distinction?

The three kinds of foods

8. The foods which increase life, energy, strength, health, joy and cheerfulness, which are savory and oleaginous, substantial and agreeable, are dear to the Sattvic.

9. The foods that are bitter, sour, saline, excessively hot, pungent, dry and burning, are liked by the Rajasic, causing pain, grief and disease.

10. The food, which is stale, tasteless, putrid, and rotten, refuse and impure, is dear to the Tamasic.

The three kinds of worship

11. That worship is Sattvic which is offered by men desiring no fruit, as enjoined in the Law, with a fixed resolve in the mind that they should merely worship.

12. That which is offered with a view to reward and for ostentation, know it to be a Rajasic worship.

13. They declare that worship to be Tamasic which is contrary to the ordinances, in which no food is distributed, which is devoid of mantras and gifts, and which is devoid of faith.

Physical Activity

14. Worshipping the Gods, the twice-born, teachers and wise men, — purity, straightforwardness, continence, and abstinence from injury- are termed the bodily austerity.

Austerity in Speech

15. The speech which causes no excitement and is true, as also pleasant, and beneficial, and the practice of sacred recitation, are said to form the austerity of speech.

Mental Austerity

16. Serenity of mind, good-heartedness, silence, self-control, purity of nature, — this is called the mental austerity.

The three kinds of Austerity according to Gunas

17. This threefold austerity, practiced by devout men with utmost faith, desiring no fruit, they call Sattvic.

18. That austerity which is practiced with the object of gaining good reception, honor, and worship, and with hypocrisy, is said to be of this t world, to be Rajasic, unstable and uncertain.

19. That austerity, which is practiced out of a foolish notion, with self-torture, or for the purpose of ruining another, is declared to be Tamasic.

The three kinds of Gift

20. That gift which is given — knowing it to be a duty to give — to one who does no service, in place and in time, and to a worthy person, that gift is held Sattvic.

21. And that gift which is given with a view to a return of the good, or looking for the fruit, or reluctantly, that gift is held to be Rajasic.

22. The gift that is given at a wrong place or time, to unworthy persons, without respect or with insult, that is declared to be Tamasic.

How to perfect the defect acts

23. "Om, Tat, Sat", this has been taught to be the triple designation of Brahman. By that were created of old the brahmanas and the Vedas and the sacrifices.

24. Therefore, with the utterance of 'Om,' are the acts of sacrifice, gift, and austerity, as enjoined in the scriptures, always begun by the students of Brahman.

25. With 'Tat,' without aiming at the fruits, are the acts of sacrifice and austerity and the various acts of gift performed by the seekers of moksha.

26. The word 'Sat' is used in the sense of reality and of goodness; and so also the word 'Sat' is used in the sense of an auspicious act.

27. Devotion to sacrifice, austerity and gift is also spoken of as 'Sat'; and even action in connection with these is called 'Sat.'

Works without faith are fruitless

28. Whatever is sacrificed, given, or done, and whatever austerity is practiced, without faith, it is called 'asat'; it is naught here or hereafter.

18 - CONCLUSION (Yoga of Liberation)

Samnyasa and Tyaga distinguished

Arjuna said:

1. Of samnyasa I desire to know the truth as also of tyaga, severally.

The Blessed Lord said:

2. Sages understand samnyasa to be the renouncement of interested works; the abandonment of the fruits of all works, the learned declare, is tyaga.

Should the ignorant perform words or not?

3. That action should be abandoned as an evil, some philosophers declare; while others (declare) that acts of sacrifice, gift and austerity should not be given up.

The ignorant should perform work

4. Learn from Me the truth about this abandonment, Arjuna; abandonment, has been declared to be of three kinds.

5. Practice of worship, gift, and austerity should not be given up; it is quite necessary; worship, gift and austerity are the

purifiers of the wise.

The obligatory works should be performed without attachment

6. But even those actions should be performed, setting aside attachment and the fruits; this is My firm and highest belief.

Tamasic and Rajasic renunciations of works

7. Verily, the abandonment of an obligatory duty is not proper; the abandonment thereof from ignorance is declared to be Tamasic.

8. Whatever act one may abandon because it is painful, from fear of bodily trouble, he practices Rajasic abandonment, and he shall obtain no fruit whatever of abandonment.

Renunciation in works is Sattvic

9. Whatever obligatory work is done merely because it ought to be done, abandoning attachment and the fruit, that abandonment is deemed to be Sattvic.

From renunciation in works to renunciation of all works

10. He hates not evil action, nor is he attached to a good one, — he who has abandoned, pervaded by Sattva, and possessed of wisdom, his doubts cut asunder.

Renunciation of fruits is alone possible for the ignorant

11. Verily, it is not possible for an embodied - being to abandon actions completely; he who abandons the fruits of actions is verily said to be an abandoner.

Effects of the two renunciations after death

12. The threefold fruit of action, — evil, good, and mixed, — accrues after death to non-abandoners, but never to abandoners.

Factors in the production of an act

13. These live factors in the accomplishment of all action, know that from Me as taught in the Sankhya which is the end of action.

14. The seat and actor and the various organs, and the several functions of various sorts, and the Divinity also, the fifth among these;

15. Whatever action a man does by the body, speech, and mind, right or the opposite, these five are its causes.

The agency of the Self is an illusion

16. Now, such being the case, verily, he who, as untrained in understanding, looks on the pure Self as the agent, that man of perverted intelligence sees not.

Realization of the non-agency of the Self leads to absolution from the effects of all works

17. He who is free from egotistic notion, whose mind is not tainted, — though he kills these creatures, he kills not, he is not bound.

The impulse to action

18. Knowledge, the object known, the knower, (form) the threefold impulse to action; the organ, the end, the agent, form the threefold basis of action.

The impulses are threefold according to the gunas

19. Knowledge and action, and the agent, are said in the science of the gunas to be of three kinds only, according to the distinction in gunas.

Three Knowledge

20. That by which a man sees the one Indestructible Reality in all beings, inseparate in the separated, — that knowledge

as Sattvic.

21. But that knowledge which, by differentiation, sees in all the creatures various entities of distinct kinds, that knowledge as Rajasic.

22. But that which clings to one single effect as if it were all, without reason, having no real object, and narrow, that is declared to be Tamasic.

Three Action

23. An action which is ordained, which is free from attachment, which is done without love or hatred by one not desirous of the fruit, that action is declared to be Sattvic.

24. But the action which is done by one longing for pleasures or done by the egotistic, costing much trouble, that is declared to be Rajasic.

25. The action, which is undertaken from delusion, without regarding the consequence, loss, injury, and ability, that is declared to be Tamasic.

Three Agent

26. Free from attachment, not given to egotism, endued with firmness and vigor, unaffected in success and failure, an agent is said to be Sattvic.

27. Passionate, desiring to attain the fruit of action, greedy, cruel, impure, subject to joy and sorrow, such an agent is said to be Rajasic.

28. Unsteady, vulgar, unbending, deceptive, wicked, indolent, desponding, and procrastinating, (such) an agent is said to be Tamasic.

Intellect and firmness are threefold accounting to gunas

29. The threefold division of intellect and firmness according to qualities, about to be taught fully and distinctively (by Me).

Three Intellect

30. That which knows action and inaction, what ought to be done and what ought not to be done, fear and absence of fear, bondage, and liberation, that intellect is Sattvic.

31. That by which one wrongly understands dharma and a-dharma, and what ought to be done and what ought not to be done, that intellect is Rajasic.

32. That which, enveloped in darkness, sees adharma as dharma and all things perverted, that intellect is Tamasic.

Three Firmness

33. The firmness, which is ever accompanied by Yoga, and by which the activities of thought, of life-breaths and sense-organs are held fast, such firmness is Sattvic.

34. But the firmness with which one holds fast to dharma and pleasures and wealth, desirous of the fruit of each on its occasion, that firmness is Rajasic.

35. That with which a stupid man does not give up sleep, fear, grief, depression, and lust, that firmness is Tamasic.

Three Pleasure

36. And now hear from Me, Arjuna, of the threefold pleasure, in which one delights by practice and surely comes to the end of pain.

37. That which is like poison at first, like nectar at the end, that pleasure is declared to be Sattvic, born of the purity of one's own mind.

38. That pleasure which arises from the contact of the sense-organ with the object, at first like nectar, in the end like poison, that is declared to be Rajasic.

39. The pleasure which at first and in the sequel is delusive of the self, arising from sleep, indolence, and heedlessness, that pleasure is declared to be Tamasic.

No man or god is free from gunas

40. There is no being on earth, or again in heaven among the Devas, that can be free from these three gunas born of Prakriti.

Duties of the four castes ordained according to nature

41. Of Brahmanas and Kshatriyas and Vaisyas, as also of Sudras the duties are divided according to the qualities born of nature.

42. Serenity, self-restraint, austerity, purity, forgiveness, and uprightness, knowledge, wisdom, faith, — these are the duties of the Brahmanas, born of nature.

43. Bravery, boldness, fortitude, promptness, not flying from battle, generosity and lordliness are the duties of the Kshatriyas, born of nature.

44. Ploughing, cattle-rearing, and trade are the duties of the Vaisyas, born of nature. And of the nature of service is the duty of the Sudra, born of nature.

Devotion to one's own duty leads to perfection

45. Devoted each to his own duty, man attains perfection; how one, devoted to one's own duty, attains success.

46. Him from whom is the evolution of (all) beings, by whom all this is pervaded, — by worship ping Him with his proper duty, man attains perfection.

47. Better is one's own duty (though) destitute of merits, than the duty of another well performed. Doing the duty ordained according to nature, one incurs no sin.

One ought not to abandon one's own duty

48. The duty born with oneself, Arjuna, though faulty, one ought not to abandon; for, all undertakings are surrounded with evil, as fire with smoke.

Perfection in Karma-Yoga leads to absolute Perfection

49. He whose reason is not attached anywhere, whose self is subdued, from whom desire has fled, he by renunciation attains the supreme state of freedom from action.

50. How he who has attained perfection reaches Brahman, that in brief learn from Me— that supreme consummation of knowledge.

The Path to absolute Perfection

51. Endued with a pure reason, controlling the self with firmness, abandoning sound and other objects, and laying aside love and hatred;

52. Resorting to a sequestered spot, eating but little, speech and body and mind subdued, always engaged in meditation and concentration, endued with dispassion;

53. Having abandoned egotism, strength, arrogance, desire, enmity, property, free from the notion of "mine,"and peaceful, he is fit for becoming Brahman.

The consummation of Knowledge attained by Devotion

54. Becoming Brahman, of serene self, he neither grieves nor desires, treating all beings alike; he attains supreme devotion to Me.

55. By Devotion he knows Me in truth, what and who I am;

then, knowing Me in truth, he forthwith enters into Me.

Devotion to the Lord by works enjoyed

56. Doing continually all actions whatsoever, taking refuge in Me, — by My Grace he reaches the eternal undecaying Abode.

57. Mentally resigning all deeds to Me, regarding Me as the Supreme, resorting to mental concentration, ever fix your heart in Me.

58. Fixing your heart in Me, you shall, by My Grace, cross over all difficulties; but if from egotism you will not hear (Me), you shall perish.

59. If, indulging egotism, you think 'I will not fight,' vain is this, your resolve; nature will constrain you.

60. Bound by your own nature, that which from delusion you do not want to do, you shall, though against your will.

61. The Lord dwells in the hearts of all beings, whirling by Maya all beings (as if) mounted on a machine.

62. Fly unto Him for refuge with all your being; by His Grace you shall obtain supreme peace (and) the eternal resting place.

63. Thus has wisdom, more secret than all that is secret, been declared to you by Me; reflect over it all and act as you please.

Devotion to the Lord is the Secret of Success in Karma-Yoga

64. Hear again My word supreme, the most secret of all; because you are My firm friend, therefore will I tell you what is good.

65. Fix your thought on Me, be devoted to Me, worship Me, do homage to Me. You shall reach Myself. The truth do I declare to you for you are dear to Me.

Right Knowledge and Renunciation

66. Abandoning all righteous deeds, seek Me as your sole Refuge; I will liberate you from all sins; do not grieve.

Qualifications for Instructions in the Gita Doctrine

67. This (which has been taught) to you is never to be taught to one who is devoid of austerities, nor to one who is not devoted, nor to one who does not do service, nor to one who speaks ill of Me.

The merit of teaching the Doctrine

68. He who with supreme devotion to Me will teach this Supreme Secret to My devotees, shall doubtless come to Me.

69. Nor is there any among men who does dearer service to Me than he; nor shall there be another on earth dearer to Me than he.

70. And he who will study this sacred dialogue of ours, by him I shall have been worshipped by the sacrifice of wisdom, I deem.

The merit of hearing the Doctrine

71. And the man also who hears, full of faith and free from malice, even he, liberated, shall attain to the happy worlds of the righteous.

The Lord assured by Arjuna oh his grasp of the Teaching

72. Has it been heard by you, Arjuna, with an attentive mind? Has the delusion of ignorance been destroyed?

Arjuna said:

73. Destroyed is delusion, and I have gained recognition through your Grace. I am firm, with doubts gone. I will do your word.

Sanjaya extols the Lord and His teaching

Sanjaya said:

74. Thus have I heard this wonderful dialogue between Arjuna and Krishna which makes the hair stand on end.

75. Through the grace of Vyasa have I heard this Supreme and most secret Yoga direct from Krishna, the Lord of Yoga, Himself declaring it.

76. O king, remembering every moment this wonderful and holy dialogue between Krishna and Arjuna, I rejoice again and again.

77. And remembering every moment the most wonderful Form of Krishna, great is my wonder, O king; and I rejoice again and again.

78. Wherever is Krishna, the Lord of Yoga, wherever is Arjuna, the archer, there fortune, victory, prosperity, and polity are established.

ABOUT THE AUTHOR

The Bhagavad Gita was written about 200BCE and originally commented by Sri Shankaracharya. Alladi Mahadeva Sastri translated the Sanskrit commentaries by Sri Shankaracharya in 1901.

Alladi Mahadeva Sastri (1861-1926) was born in Pudur, India. Being well studied in Sanskrit and English, he was able to recite the Vedas at a young age.

In 1891 he became the first Curator of the Oriental Library and began translating the classic Bhagavat Gita commentaries by Sri Shankaracharya into English. He was praised by Swami Vivekananda for this commendable work. Sastri book was published in 1901.

The work is comparable, if not better, to other translations and gives precise translations of difficult Sanskrit words.

In editing this book, I have removed all the commentaries and kept just the sloka translations. Also removed the 'old English' to make the verses more palatable to the modern English. This allows for fluid reading of passages.

Printed in Great Britain
by Amazon

18323858R00062